Aunt Phil's Trunk

Student Workbook

for

The Spell of the Yukon and Other Verses

Poetry by
ROBERT SERVICE

Curriculum by
LAUREL DOWNING BILL

Student Workbook

for

The Spell of the Yukon
And Other Verses

Poetry By
Robert Service

Curriculum By
Laurel Downing Bill

Special thanks to Nicole Cruz for her assitance in makng this student workbook and its accompanying teacher guide for *The Spell of the Yukon and Other Verses*

Aunt Phil's Trunk LLC
Anchorage, Alaska
www.AuntPhilsTrunk.com

ISBN: 978-1-940479-19-4

Instructions for using Aunt Phil's Trunk
Proudly Presents
The Spell of the Yukon
And Other Verses
Curriculum

This curriculum is designed to be used as part of a ninth- or tenth-grade Language Arts curriculum. In each lesson, you will learn new vocabulary words, answer discussion questions, and consider how concepts such as rhyme scheme, theme, tone, and imagery are used in each poem. At the conclusion of every lesson, you will complete an enrichment activity to encourage deeper interaction with the poem, as well as practice writing your own poetry.

After reading and analyzing more than 30 of Robert Service's famous poems, you will read two chapters about his life and complete a final lesson analyzing how his life events impacted his poetry.

I hope you enjoy this journey into the life and poetry of Robert Service.

GRADING: Rubric grids, located on pages 123 and 124, will be used to grade the quality of your work. After you complete each lesson, check the grids to see if you think your work is acceptable or outstanding!

TABLE OF CONTENTS

TABLE OF CONTENTS (Con't.)

Robert Service Cabin, Dawson

THE SPELL OF THE YUKON

LESSON 1: THE LAND GOD FORGOT

VOCABULARY

Look for these words in your reading:

Desolate – abandoned
Gaunt – grim or forbidding
Insensate – lacking humane feelings
Abysmal – extremely bad

READING

Read: To C.M., the Introduction and "The Land God Forgot" (Pages 3-10)

DISCUSSION QUESTIONS

1) Who was C.M.? Why did Robert Service dedicate the *Spell of the Yukon and Other Verses* to her?

_____

_____

_____

2) Did Robert Service ever return to the Yukon cabin that he wrote about in "Good-bye Little Cabin" after he wrote the poem in 1912? What happened to that cabin?

_____

_____

_____

3) In your own words, describe the land that Robert Service wrote about in "The Land God Forgot."

_____

_____

_____

4) Have you ever been to a place that resembles the land in "The Land God Forgot"? If so, explain why the poem reminds you of that place.

_____

_____

_____

_____

FAVORITE LINE

What is your favorite line from "The Land God Forgot." Why?

_____
_____
_____
_____
_____
_____

ENRICHMENT ACTIVITY

Using some of the words that you used to describe the land in Discussion Question 3, write your own poem describing a place that you have been or an imaginary setting.

_____
_____
_____
_____
_____
_____
_____
_____
_____
_____
_____
_____
_____
_____
_____
_____
_____
_____
_____
_____
_____
_____
_____
_____

_____
_____
_____
_____
_____
_____
_____
_____
_____
_____
_____
_____
_____
_____
_____
_____
_____
_____
_____
_____
_____
_____
_____
_____

LESSON 1: THE LAND GOD FORGOT

Discussion Questions _____ (10 pts. per question – possible 40 pts.)
Favorite Quote _____ (possible 10 pts.)

Enrichment Activity
    Originality and Creativity   _____ (possible 10 pts.)
    Follows Directions   _____ (possible 10 pts.)
    Language and Style   _____ (possible 10 pts.)
    Composition is Neat   _____ (possible 10 pts.)
    Grammar and Spelling   _____ (possible 10 pts.)

Total Points _____

THE SPELL OF THE YUKON

LESSON 2: THE SPELL OF THE YUKON

VOCABULARY

Look for these words in your reading:

Shun – to avoid purposely
Caribou – a large animal of the deer family
Bludgeons – beats, thrashes
Luring – to tempt or attract

READING

Read: "The Spell of the Yukon" (Pages 11-13)

DISCUSSION QUESTIONS

1) What appears to draw the narrator to the Yukon at the beginning of the poem?

_____

_____

_____

2) What draws the narrator to the Yukon at the end of the poem?

_____

_____

3) Does the narrator love everything about the Yukon? Explain your answer.

_____

_____

_____

4) Does the narrator live in the Yukon? How can you tell?

_____

_____

_____

5) If you had to describe the moral or lesson of "The Spell of the Yukon," what would it be?

_____

_____

_____

FAVORITE LINE

What is your favorite line from "The Spell of the Yukon"? Why?

_____
_____
_____
_____
_____
_____

ENRICHMENT ACTIVITY

Robert Service used an alternate rhyme scheme in "The Spell of the Yukon" making it very easy to read. We also call this the ABAB pattern because the last word in each line of the stanza rhymes with the last word in the alternating line. For example:

There's gold, and it's haunting and haunting; (A)
It's luring me on as of old; (B)
Yet it isn't the gold that I'm wanting (A)
So much as just finding the gold. (B)

Write your own poem on the next page using an alternate rhyme scheme.

_____
_____
_____
_____
_____
_____
_____
_____
_____
_____
_____
_____
_____
_____
_____
_____

_____
_____
_____
_____
_____
_____
_____
_____
_____
_____
_____
_____
_____
_____
_____
_____
_____
_____
_____
_____
_____
_____
_____
_____
_____

LESSON 2: THE SPELL OF THE YUKON

Discussion Questions _____ (10 pts. per question – possible 50 pts.)
Favorite Quote (No points for this lesson)

Enrichment Activity
    Originality and Creativity   _____ (possible 10 pts.)
    Follows Directions   _____ (possible 10 pts.)
    Language and Style   _____ (possible 10 pts.)
    Composition is Neat   _____ (possible 10 pts.)
    Grammar and Spelling   _____ (possible 10 pts.)

Total Points _____

THE SPELL OF THE YUKON

LESSON 3: THE HEART OF THE SOURDOUGH

VOCABULARY

Look for these words in your reading:

Sourdough – Alaskan term for a person who has spent at least one winter north of the Arctic Circle

Tundra – a treeless plain especially of arctic regions having a permanently frozen layer below the surface

Defy – openly resist or refuse to obey

Flouted – ignore in a disrespectful way

READING

Read: "The Heart of the Sourdough" (Pages 14-15)

DISCUSSION QUESTIONS

1) According to the narrator, what is important to the heart of a sourdough?

_____

_____

_____

2) What battle does the narrator describe in the poem? Who will win the fight?

_____

_____

_____

3) What do you think the narrator meant by the line below?
"I long for a whiff of bacon and beans, a snug shakedown in the snow; a trail to break, and a life at stake, and another bout with the foe."

_____

_____

_____

4) Does "The Heart of the Sourdough" remind you of another poem or story? If so, which one?

_____

_____

_____

FAVORITE LINE

What is your favorite line from "The Heart of the Sourdough"? Why?

_____

_____

_____

_____

_____

_____

ENRICHMENT ACTIVITY

How would you describe your heart? What people, places and things are most important to you? Make a list of 5-10 things. Write a poem using your list.

_____

_____

_____

_____

_____

_____

_____

_____

_____

_____

_____

_____

_____

_____

_____

_____

_____

_____

_____

_____

_____

_____
_____
_____
_____
_____
_____
_____
_____
_____
_____
_____
_____
_____
_____
_____
_____
_____
_____
_____
_____
_____
_____
_____
_____

LESSON 3: THE HEART OF THE SOURDOUGH

Discussion Questions _____ (10 pts. per question – possible 40 pts.)
Favorite Quote _____ (possible 10 pts.)

Enrichment Activity
    Originality and Creativity   _____ (possible 10 pts.)
    Follows Directions   _____ (possible 10 pts.)
    Language and Style   _____ (possible 10 pts.)
    Composition is Neat   _____ (possible 10 pts.)
    Grammar and Spelling   _____ (possible 10 pts.)

Total Points _____

THE SPELL OF THE YUKON

LESSON 4: THE THREE VOICES

VOCABULARY

Look for these words in your reading:

Aloft – at a great height
Anthem – a song or hymn of praise or gladness
Sally – an excursion
Unfurled – to unfold

READING

Read: "The Three Voices" (Page 16)

DISCUSSION QUESTIONS

1) Who do the three voices belong to?

_____
_____
_____

2) What do the three voices tell the narrator?

_____
_____
_____
_____

3) What does the narrator long for?

_____
_____
_____

4) Can you relate to the narrator's experience on the beach? If so, how?

_____
_____
_____
_____
_____
_____

FAVORITE LINE

What is your favorite line from "The Three Voices"? Why?

_____

_____

_____

_____

_____

_____

ENRICHMENT ACTIVITY

Robert Service often spent time walking outdoors with pen and paper to write about whatever he saw and experienced. Spend some time outdoors writing down what you see, smell, hear, touch, etc. Write a poem that shares this experience.

_____

_____

_____

_____

_____

_____

_____

_____

_____

_____

_____

_____

_____

_____

_____

_____

_____

_____

_____

_____

_____

_____

_____

_____

_____

_____

_____

_____

_____

_____

_____

_____

_____

_____

_____

_____

_____

_____

_____

_____

_____

_____

_____

_____

_____

_____

_____

_____

_____

LESSON 4: THE THREE VOICES

Discussion Questions _____ (10 pts. per question – possible 40 pts.)
Favorite Quote _____ (possible 10 pts.)

Enrichment Activity
    Originality and Creativity   _____ (possible 10 pts.)
    Follows Directions   _____ (possible 10 pts.)
    Language and Style   _____ (possible 10 pts.)
    Composition is Neat   _____ (possible 10 pts.)
    Grammar and Spelling   _____ (possible 10 pts.)

Total Points _____

THE SPELL OF THE YUKON

LESSON 5: THE LAW OF THE YUKON

VOCABULARY

Look for these words in your reading:

Grit – firmness of mind or spirit
Enervate – lacking physical, mental or moral vigor
Manifold – of many and various kinds
Mettle – strength of spirit

READING

Read: "The Law of the Yukon" (Pages 17-21)

DISCUSSION QUESTIONS

1) What is the law of the Yukon?

_____

_____

_____

2) What happens to the "Weak"?

_____

_____

_____

3) According to the narrator, what does the Yukon dream of?

_____

_____

_____

4) Why do you think it takes grit to survive in the Yukon?

_____

_____

_____

FAVORITE LINE

What is your favorite line from "The Law of the Yukon"? Why?

_____
_____
_____
_____
_____
_____

ENRICHMENT ACTIVITY

In "The Law of the Yukon," Robert Service used a technique called personification. Personification means that the poet gives human qualities or emotions to objects or ideas. He wrote about a place that was able to think, feel, dream and even cause harm toward its inhabitants. Write a poem about a place that is of special importance to you using personification.

_____
_____
_____
_____
_____
_____
_____
_____
_____
_____
_____
_____
_____
_____
_____
_____
_____
_____
_____
_____
_____
_____

_____
_____
_____
_____
_____
_____
_____
_____
_____
_____
_____
_____
_____
_____
_____
_____
_____
_____
_____
_____
_____
_____
_____
_____
_____

LESSON 5: THE LAW OF THE YUKON

Discussion Questions _____ (10 pts. per question – possible 40 pts.)
Favorite Quote _____ (possible 10 pts.)

Enrichment Activity
   Originality and Creativity   _____ (possible 10 pts.)
    Follows Directions   _____ (possible 10 pts.)
    Language and Style   _____ (possible 10 pts.)
    Composition is Neat   _____ (possible 10 pts.)
    Grammar and Spelling   _____ (possible 10 pts.)

Total Points _____

THE SPELL OF THE YUKON

LESSON 6: THE PARSON'S SON

VOCABULARY

Look for these words in your reading:

Toiled – long strenuous fatiguing effort
Squandered – spent extravagantly or foolishly
Malamute – a sled dog of northern North America
Fiendish – extremely cruel or wicked

READING

Read: "The Parson's Son" (Pages 22-25)

DISCUSSION QUESTIONS

1) How would you describe the Parson's son? What did he look like?

_____

_____

_____

2) How many years did he spend in the Yukon? Why did he go there?

_____

_____

_____

3) What happened to the Parson's son?

_____

_____

_____

4) At the end of the poem we learn that the Parson's son died alone on his bunk. Judging from his song, do you think that he had a happy life in the Yukon? Why or why not?

_____

_____

_____

FAVORITE LINE

What is your favorite line from "The Parson's Son"? Why?

_____
_____
_____
_____
_____

ENRICHMENT ACTIVITY

Imagine that you are an old man or woman at the end of your life. Write a song that summarizes your life. Where did you go? What did you spend your life doing? Who was important to you?

_____
_____
_____
_____
_____
_____
_____
_____
_____
_____
_____
_____
_____
_____
_____
_____
_____
_____
_____
_____
_____
_____
_____
_____

_____

_____

_____

_____

_____

_____

_____

_____

_____

_____

_____

_____

_____

_____

_____

_____

_____

_____

_____

_____

_____

_____

_____

_____

LESSON 6: THE PARSON'S LAW

Discussion Questions _____ (10 pts. per question – possible 40 pts.)
Favorite Quote _____ (possible 10 pts.)

Enrichment Activity
    Originality and Creativity   _____ (possible 10 pts.)
    Follows Directions   _____ (possible 10 pts.)
    Language and Style   _____ (possible 10 pts.)
    Composition is Neat   _____ (possible 10 pts.)
    Grammar and Spelling   _____ (possible 10 pts.)

Total Points _____

THE SPELL OF THE YUKON

LESSON 7: THE CALL OF THE WILD

VOCABULARY

Look for these words in your reading:

Grandeur – awe-inspiring magnificence
Desolation – lifeless land
Hearken – listen; attend to
Veneer – a superficial or deceptively attractive appearance, display or effect

READING

Read: "The Call of the Wild" (Pages 26-28)

DISCUSSION QUESTIONS

1) What is the theme (central idea) of "The Call of the Wild"?

_____

_____

_____

2) What are five words you would use to describe a person that hears the call of the wild?

_____

_____

_____

3) What are some differences that you noticed in the style of this poem compared to the other Robert Service poems that you have studied so far?

_____

_____

_____

4) What feelings and emotions did this poem elicit in you? Go back and reread the poem. Can you pinpoint specific elements, words, or lines that caused these emotions?

_____

_____

_____

FAVORITE LINE

What is your favorite line from "The Call of the Wild"? Why?

_____

_____

_____

_____

_____

ENRICHMENT ACTIVITY

Questions can be used as a literary device to create dramatic effect, persuade the audience or cause the reader to ponder an important theme. Write your own question poem that imitates the style of "The Call of the Wild."

_____

_____

_____

_____

_____

_____

_____

_____

_____

_____

_____

_____

_____

_____

_____

_____

_____

_____

_____

_____

_____

_____

_____

_____
_____
_____
_____
_____
_____
_____
_____
_____
_____
_____
_____
_____
_____
_____
_____
_____
_____
_____
_____
_____
_____
_____
_____

LESSON 7: THE CALL OF THE WILD

Discussion Questions _____ (10 pts. per question – possible 40 pts.)
Favorite Quote _____ (possible 10 pts.)

Enrichment Activity
    Originality and Creativity   _____ (possible 10 pts.)
    Follows Directions   _____ (possible 10 pts.)
    Language and Style   _____ (possible 10 pts.)
    Composition is Neat   _____ (possible 10 pts.)
    Grammar and Spelling   _____ (possible 10 pts.)

Total Points _____

THE SPELL OF THE YUKON

LESSON 8: THE LONE TRAIL

VOCABULARY

Look for these words in your reading:

Fain – in a willing manner
Drouth – long period of dry weather
Anguish – extreme pain or distress of the body or mind
Mirage – an optical illusion caused by atmospheric conditions, especially the appearance of a sheet of water in a desert or on a hot road caused by the refraction of light from the sky by heated air

READING

Read: "The Lone Trail" (Pages 29-30)

DISCUSSION QUESTIONS

1) Why do you think Robert Service titled this poem, "The Lone Trail"? Support your answer with a line from the poem.

_____
_____
_____

2) According to the narrator, why would some choose the lone trail over the other trails?

_____
_____
_____

3) Other than the words lone and trail, what word do you notice is used many times in this poem? Why do you think Robert Service used that word so often in the poem?

_____
_____
_____

4) Reread "The Lone Trail." How can you relate it to your own life?

_____
_____
_____
_____

FAVORITE LINE

What is your favorite line from "The Lone Trail"? Why?

_____

_____

_____

_____

_____

ENRICHMENT ACTIVITY

Anaphora refers to a literary technique where successive lines begin with the same word or phrase. Poets have used this technique for centuries to create rhythm and intensify emotion. Anaphora has been used in a lot of religious writing, including biblical psalms, and in romantic writing, such as works by William Shakespeare. Find at least three poems that use anaphora and write the titles below.

1) _____

2) _____

3) _____

Compose a poem using anaphora.

_____

_____

_____

_____

_____

_____

_____

_____

_____

_____

_____

_____

_____

_____

_____

_____

_____

_____

_____

_____

_____

_____

_____

_____

_____

_____

_____

_____

_____

_____

_____

_____

_____

_____

_____

_____

_____

_____

_____

_____

_____

_____

LESSON 8: THE LONE TRAIL

Discussion Questions _____ (10 pts. per question – possible 40 pts.)
Favorite Quote _____ (possible 10 pts.)

Enrichment Activity
    Originality and Creativity   _____ (possible 10 pts.)
    Follows Directions   _____ (possible 10 pts.)
    Language and Style   _____ (possible 10 pts.)
    Composition is Neat   _____ (possible 10 pts.)
    Grammar and Spelling   _____ (possible 10 pts.)

Total Points _____

THE SPELL OF THE YUKON

LESSON 9: THE PINES

VOCABULARY

Look for these words in your reading:

Niggard – stingy or ungenerous
Gelid – extremely cold
Aeons – a very long period of time
Legion – large military force

READING

Read: "The Pines" (Pages 31-32)

DISCUSSION QUESTIONS

1) A stanza is a group of lines within a poem that are typically set apart by a blank line. Reread the first stanza of the poem. How does it set the mood for the rest of the poem?

_____

_____

_____

2) What literary technique do you recognize in the third stanza of "The Pines"?

_____

_____

_____

3) What are five words that can be used to describe this poem? Some examples are: dark, gloomy or woods.

_____

_____

_____

4) Judging by the first nine poems that we've studied, what topics and themes did Robert Service often write about?

_____

_____

_____

FAVORITE LINE

What is your favorite line from "The Pines"? Why?

_____

_____

_____

_____

_____

ENRICHMENT ACTIVITY

Write a poem consisting of at least four stanzas that contain the words you chose in Discussion Question 3.

_____

_____

_____

_____

_____

_____

_____

_____

_____

_____

_____

_____

_____

_____

_____

_____

_____

_____

_____

_____

_____

_____

_____

_____

_____

_____

_____

_____
_____
_____
_____
_____
_____
_____
_____
_____
_____
_____
_____
_____
_____
_____
_____
_____
_____
_____
_____
_____
_____
_____

LESSON 9: THE PINES

Discussion Questions _____ (10 pts. per question – possible 40 pts.)
Favorite Quote _____ (possible 10 pts.)

Enrichment Activity
    Originality and Creativity   _____ (possible 10 pts.)
    Follows Directions   _____ (possible 10 pts.)
    Language and Style   _____ (possible 10 pts.)
    Composition is Neat   _____ (possible 10 pts.)
    Grammar and Spelling   _____ (possible 10 pts.)

Total Points _____

Spell of the Yukon Vocabulary
Crossword Puzzle I

Read the Across and Down clues and fill in the blank boxes that match the number on the clues

ACROSS

1 A song or hymn of praise or gladness
4 A very long period of time
6 Lacking physical, mental or moral vigor
8 Spent extravagantly or foolishly
11 In a willing manner
12 A sled dog of northern North America
13 Abandoned
14 Large military force
15 Lacking humane feelings
17 Long period of dry weather
21 A large animal of the deer family
23 Beats, thrashes
24 Listen; attend to
26 Awe-inspiring magnificence
27 Grim or forbidding
30 Firmness of mind or spirit
31 A superficial or deceptively attractive appearance, display or effect
32 Ignore in a disrespectful way
33 Openly resist or refuse to obey
34 To avoid purposely

DOWN

2 A treeless plain especially of arctic regions having permanently frozen layer below the surface
3 Long strenuous fatiguing effort
5 To unfold
7 Lifeless land
8 Alaskan term for a person who has spent at least one winter north of the Arctic Circle
9 Extremely cruel or wicked
10 An excursion
12 Of many and various kinds
16 Stingy or ungenerous
18 An optical illusion caused by atmospheric conditions, especially the appearance of a sheet of water in a desert or on a hot road caused by the refraction of light from the sky by heated air
19 Extremely bad
20 Strength of spirit
22 Extreme pain or distress of the body or mind
25 To tempt or attract
28 At a great height
29 Extremely cold

Spell of the Yukon Vocabulary
Crossword Puzzle I

Read the Across and Down clues and fill in the blank boxes that match the number on the clues

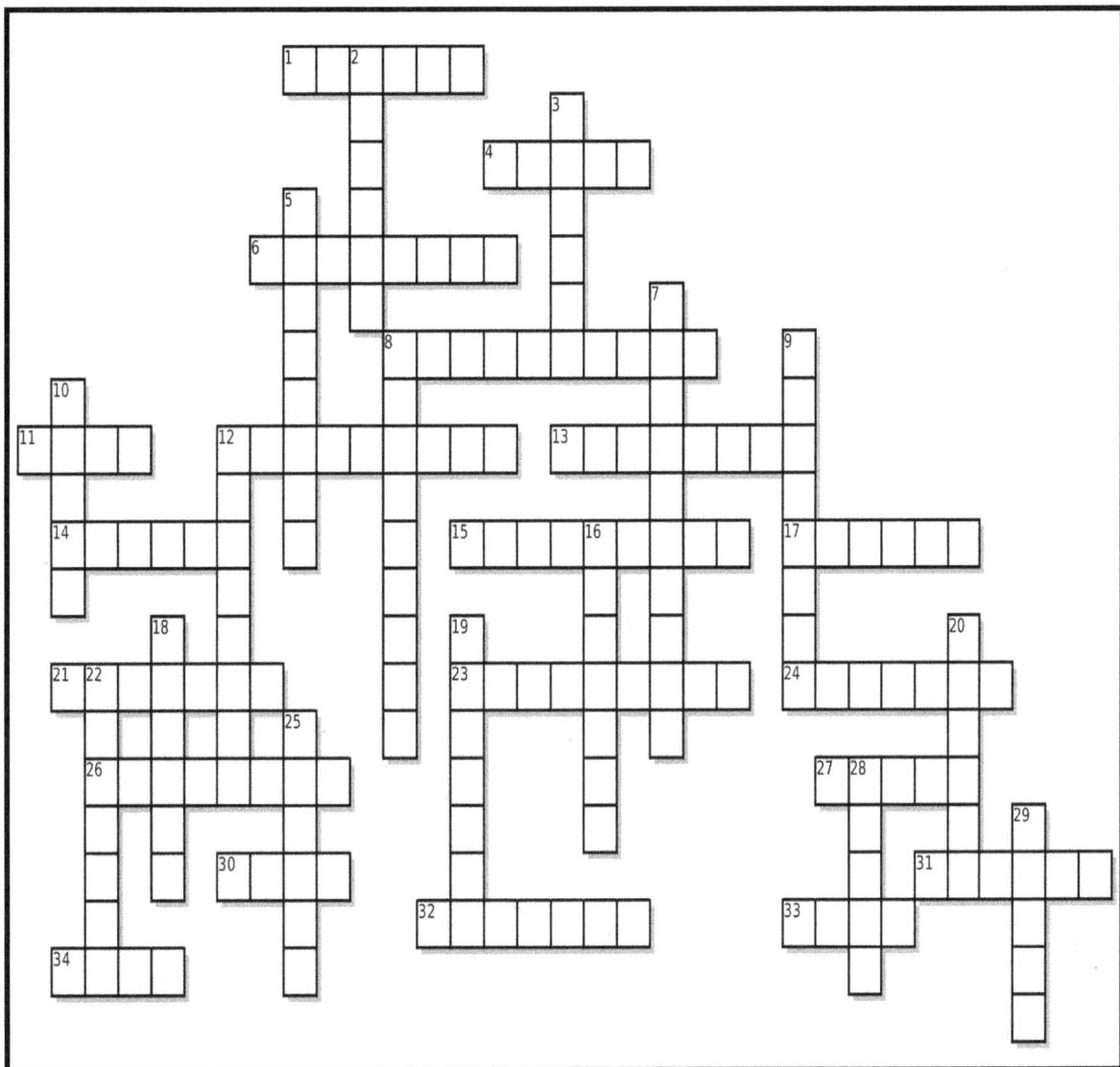

THE SPELL OF THE YUKON

LESSON 10: THE LURE OF LITTLE VOICES

VOCABULARY

Look for these words in your reading:

Stark – desolate
Sentinel – a guard whose job is to stand and keep watch
Mandate – an authoritative command
Comrade – close friend or associate

READING

Read: "The Lure of Little Voices" (Pages 33-34)

DISCUSSION QUESTIONS

1) Who is the audience of this poem? How do you know?

_____

_____

_____

2) What are the little voices telling the speaker?

_____

_____

_____

3) Has the speaker been to the place that the little voices are calling him to? Explain your answer.

_____

_____

_____

4) In poetry, we can often read between the lines to make logical assumptions about what the poet is trying to get across to the reader. This is called an inference. Reread the poem and see what inference you can make.

_____

_____

_____

FAVORITE LINE

What is your favorite line from "The Lure of Little Voices"? Why?

_____

_____

_____

_____

_____

ENRICHMENT ACTIVITY

Write a poem in response to "The Lure of Little Voices" from the point of view of either:
   1) The person that the speaker is speaking to in the poem.
   2) The speaker. Respond to the little voices that are luring him to the wild.

_____

_____

_____

_____

_____

_____

_____

_____

_____

_____

_____

_____

_____

_____

_____

_____

_____

_____

_____

_____

_____

_____

_____

_____

_____
_____
_____
_____
_____
_____
_____
_____
_____
_____
_____
_____
_____
_____
_____
_____
_____
_____
_____
_____
_____
_____
_____
_____
_____

LESSON 10: THE LURE OF LITTLE VOICES

Discussion Questions _____ (10 pts. per question – possible 40 pts.)
Favorite Quote _____ (possible 10 pts.)

Enrichment Activity
    Originality and Creativity   _____ (possible 10 pts.)
    Follows Directions   _____ (possible 10 pts.)
    Language and Style   _____ (possible 10 pts.)
    Composition is Neat   _____ (possible 10 pts.)
    Grammar and Spelling   _____ (possible 10 pts.)

Total Points _____

THE SPELL OF THE YUKON

LESSON 11: THE SONG OF THE WAGE-SLAVE

VOCABULARY

Look for these words in your reading:

Shirk – to avoid something one ought to do
Repentant – state of repentance (feeling sorry for one's sins)
Wrought – work
Blaspheme – speak irreverently about God or sacred things

READING

Read: "The Song of the Wage-Slave" (Pages 35-37)

DISCUSSION QUESTIONS

1) Briefly summarize "The Song of the Wage-Slave"?

_____
_____
_____

2) Who is the wage-slave? Who is the Big Boss?

_____
_____
_____

3) What does the wage-slave want?

_____
_____
_____

4) Can you relate to this poem in any way? Explain why or why not.

_____
_____
_____

FAVORITE LINE

What is your favorite line from "The Song of a Wage-Slave"? Why?

_____
_____
_____
_____
_____

ENRICHMENT ACTIVITY

There are many things that we should look at when analyzing poetry. Three questions we should always ask are:

   1) What is the poet saying?

   2) What inferences can I make? (Read between the lines.)

   3) How can I relate to this poem?

Choose a poem written by someone other than Robert Service, and then write your answers to the three questions above.

Name of Poem:_____

Author: _____

_____
_____
_____
_____
_____
_____
_____
_____
_____
_____
_____
_____
_____
_____
_____
_____
_____
_____
_____

_____

_____

_____

_____

_____

_____

_____

_____

_____

_____

_____

_____

_____

_____

_____

_____

_____

_____

_____

_____

_____

_____

_____

_____

_____

_____

_____

_____

LESSON 11: THE SONG OF THE WAGE-SLAVE

Discussion Questions _____ (10 pts. per question – possible 40 pts.)
Favorite Quote _____ (possible 10 pts.)

Enrichment Activity _____ (possible 50 pts.)

Total Points _____

THE SPELL OF THE YUKON

LESSON 12: GRIN

VOCABULARY

Look for these words in your reading:

Clout – influence
Cultivate – try to acquire or develop (a quality, sentiment or skill)
Rebuff – to refuse or check sharply
Cuff – to strike with an open hand

READING

Read: "Grin" (Pages 38-39)

DISCUSSION QUESTIONS

1) What is the theme of "Grin"?

_____

_____

_____

2) Reading poetry out loud can often allow us to hear things and see things that we didn't notice while reading in our heads. Reread "Grin" out loud. What differences do you notice about how the poem sounds, how it is structured and what the poet is saying?

_____

_____

_____

3) What adversity is the speaker referring to in this poem?

_____

_____

_____

4) What do you think about the speaker's advice? Do you agree or disagree?

_____

_____

_____

FAVORITE LINE

What is your favorite line from "Grin"? Why?

_____
_____
_____
_____
_____

ENRICHMENT ACTIVITY

Consider what advice you would give to a friend that is dealing with a difficult situation. What word would you use to represent this advice? Write a poem using this word as your title, and then see how many times you can include the word in your poem.

_____
_____
_____
_____
_____
_____
_____
_____
_____
_____
_____
_____
_____
_____
_____
_____
_____
_____
_____
_____
_____
_____
_____
_____
_____
_____

_____
_____
_____
_____
_____
_____
_____
_____
_____
_____
_____
_____
_____
_____
_____
_____
_____
_____
_____
_____
_____
_____
_____
_____

LESSON 12: GRIN

Discussion Questions _____ (10 pts. per question – possible 40 pts.)
Favorite Quote _____ (possible 10 pts.)

Enrichment Activity
    Originality and Creativity   _____ (possible 10 pts.)
    Follows Directions   _____ (possible 10 pts.)
    Language and Style   _____ (possible 10 pts.)
    Composition is Neat   _____ (possible 10 pts.)
    Grammar and Spelling   _____ (possible 10 pts.)

Total Points _____

THE SPELL OF THE YUKON

LESSON 13: THE SHOOTING OF DAN MCGREW

VOCABULARY

Look for these words in your reading:

Dreary – dismal or gloomy
Banished – to drive away
Ghastly – intensely unpleasant
Hooch – a strong alcoholic drink

READING

Read: "The Shooting of Dan McGrew" (Pages 40-43)

DISCUSSION QUESTIONS

1) Who is Dan McGrew? Who is Lou?

_____

_____

_____

2) Who is the third character in the poem? Why does he want to "repay" Dan McGrew?

_____

_____

_____

3) What pictures come to mind as you read this poem? Which words or lines inspire these images?

_____

_____

_____

4) Do you think that it was necessary for Robert Service to explain what the corpse looked like in such detail? How would the poem be different without this imagery?

_____

_____

_____

FAVORITE LINE

What is your favorite line from "The Shooting of Dan McGrew"? Why?

_____
_____
_____
_____

ENRICHMENT ACTIVITY

"The Shooting of Dan McGrew" is one of Robert Service's most well-known poems. It even inspired a movie and a novel. Write a poem that is based on your favorite movie or novel. You can use a single scene or the entire plot as your inspiration. When your poem is finished, read it to a friend or classmate, and see if they can guess which movie or book inspired your poem.

_____
_____
_____
_____
_____
_____
_____
_____
_____
_____
_____
_____
_____
_____
_____
_____
_____
_____
_____
_____
_____
_____

_____

_____

_____

_____

_____

_____

_____

_____

_____

_____

_____

_____

_____

_____

_____

_____

_____

_____

_____

_____

_____

_____

_____

_____

LESSON 13: THE SHOOTING OF DAN MCGREW

Discussion Questions _____ (10 pts. per question – possible 40 pts.)
Favorite Quote _____ (possible 10 pts.)

Enrichment Activity
    Originality and Creativity   _____ (possible 10 pts.)
    Follows Directions   _____ (possible 10 pts.)
    Language and Style   _____ (possible 10 pts.)
    Composition is Neat   _____ (possible 10 pts.)
    Grammar and Spelling   _____ (possible 10 pts.)

Total Points _____

47

THE SPELL OF THE YUKON

LESSON 14: THE CREMATION OF SAM MCGEE

VOCABULARY

Look for these words in your reading:

Marge – edge
Stern – severity of nature or manner
Loathed – dislike greatly
Derelict – abandoned ship

READING

Read: "The Cremation of Sam McGee" (Pages 44-47)

DISCUSSION QUESTIONS

1) How did Sam McGee die? Who cremated him? Why?

_____
_____
_____

2) How does the speaker describe the Arctic?

_____
_____
_____

3) What do you think is the theme of this poem?

_____
_____
_____

4) What do you think about the ending of the poem? Did you look at the poem differently after reading the ending? Explain your answer.

_____
_____
_____

FAVORITE LINE

What is your favorite line from "The Cremation of Sam McGee"? Why?

_____

_____

_____

_____

_____

ENRICHMENT ACTIVITY

In "The Cremation of Sam McGee," Robert Service adds humor to the sensitive subject of mortality and death. Write your own funny poem on any topic.

_____

_____

_____

_____

_____

_____

_____

_____

_____

_____

_____

_____

_____

_____

_____

_____

_____

_____

_____

_____

_____

_____

_____

_____

_____

_____
_____
_____
_____
_____
_____
_____
_____
_____
_____
_____
_____
_____
_____
_____
_____
_____
_____
_____
_____
_____
_____
_____
_____
_____
_____
_____

LESSON 14: THE CREMATION OF SAM MCGEE

Discussion Questions _____ (10 pts. per question – possible 40 pts.)
Favorite Quote _____ (possible 10 pts.)

Enrichment Activity
    Originality and Creativity   _____ (possible 10 pts.)
    Follows Directions   _____ (possible 10 pts.)
    Language and Style   _____ (possible 10 pts.)
    Composition is Neat   _____ (possible 10 pts.)
    Grammar and Spelling   _____ (possible 10 pts.)

Total Points _____

THE SPELL OF THE YUKON

LESSON 15: MY MADONNA

VOCABULARY

Look for these words in your reading:

Haled – compel (someone) to go
Bade – requested to come
Connoisseur – a person qualified to act as a judge in matters of taste and appreciation
Halo – a disk or circle of light shown surrounding or above the head of a saint or holy person to represent their holiness

READING

Read: "My Madonna" (Page 48)

DISCUSSION QUESTIONS

1) Who is the speaker? What does he do?

_____

_____

_____

2) Who is "Madonna" in this poem? Do you think that the connoisseur correctly identified the woman in the painting? Why or why not?

_____

_____

_____

3) What do you notice about the structure of the poem?

_____

_____

_____

4) How would you describe the mood of this poem?

_____

_____

_____

FAVORITE LINE

What is your favorite line from "My Madonna"? Why?

_____
_____
_____
_____
_____

ENRICHMENT ACTIVITY

The term "Madonna," when referring to a picture or statue of Mary, dates back to the 17th century, often referencing works from the Italian Renaissance. See if you can find an example of a Madonna painting that fits the description of the poem (halo, babe at her breast, etc.). Search in art books at your local library or online. Write a poem about what you see in that painting.

_____
_____
_____
_____
_____
_____
_____
_____
_____
_____
_____
_____
_____
_____
_____
_____
_____
_____
_____
_____
_____
_____
_____
_____

_____
_____
_____
_____
_____
_____
_____
_____
_____
_____
_____
_____
_____
_____
_____
_____
_____
_____
_____
_____
_____
_____
_____
_____
_____
_____

LESSON 15: MY MADONNA

Discussion Questions _____ (10 pts. per question – possible 40 pts.)
Favorite Quote _____ (possible 10 pts.)

Enrichment Activity
    Originality and Creativity   _____ (possible 10 pts.)
    Follows Directions   _____ (possible 10 pts.)
    Language and Style   _____ (possible 10 pts.)
    Composition is Neat   _____ (possible 10 pts.)
    Grammar and Spelling   _____ (possible 10 pts.)

Total Points _____

THE SPELL OF THE YUKON
LESSON 16: UNFORGOTTEN

VOCABULARY

Look for these words in your reading:

Garret – a room or unfinished part of a house just under the roof
Drear – having nothing likely to provide cheer or comfort
Toils – exhausting work
Seer – a person who can supposedly see into the future

READING

Read: "Unforgotten" (Page 49)

DISCUSSION QUESTIONS

1) Describe the woman in the poem.

_____
_____
_____

2) Describe the man in the poem.

_____
_____
_____

3) Why do you think the poem was titled "Unforgotten"?

_____
_____
_____

4) "Unforgotten" is written in enclosed rhyme scheme (ABBA). The first and fourth line of each stanza rhyme, and the second and third stanza rhyme. Copy the first stanza below and label the first and fourth line A, and the second and third line B.

_____
_____
_____
_____

FAVORITE LINE

What is your favorite line from "Unforgotten"? Why?

_____

_____

_____

_____

_____

ENRICHMENT ACTIVITY

Could you picture the woman fairer than lilies and the man who toils in a dark garret as you read the poem? If not, read the poem again and try to picture them. Write three stanzas to add to the poem that include a description of the images that you see of the man and woman as you read. Follow the rhyme pattern of this poem (ABBA).

_____

_____

_____

_____

_____

_____

_____

_____

_____

_____

_____

_____

_____

_____

_____

_____

_____

_____

_____

_____

_____

_____

_____

_____
_____
_____
_____
_____
_____
_____
_____
_____
_____
_____
_____
_____
_____
_____
_____
_____
_____
_____
_____
_____
_____
_____
_____

LESSON 16: UNFORGOTTEN

Discussion Questions _____ (10 pts. per question – possible 40 pts.)
Favorite Quote _____ (possible 10 pts.)

Enrichment Activity
    Originality and Creativity   _____ (possible 10 pts.)
    Follows Directions   _____ (possible 10 pts.)
    Language and Style   _____ (possible 10 pts.)
    Composition is Neat   _____ (possible 10 pts.)
    Grammar and Spelling   _____ (possible 10 pts.)

Total Points _____

THE SPELL OF THE YUKON

LESSON 17: THE RECKONING

VOCABULARY

Look for these words in your reading:

Reckoning – a settling of accounts
Terrapin – small edible turtle

READING

Read: "The Reckoning" (Pages 50-51)

DISCUSSION QUESTIONS

1) What is the theme of "The Reckoning"?

_____
_____
_____

2) Did you notice the use of symbolism in this poem? If not, read it again. What does "the bill" symbolize?

_____
_____
_____

3) If you had to give an alternate title to this poem, what would it be?

_____
_____
_____

4) How would you describe the tone of this poem (examples: pessimistic, serious, playful)? Explain your answer.

_____
_____
_____

FAVORITE LINE

What is your favorite line from "The Reckoning"? Why?

_____

_____

_____

_____

_____

ENRICHMENT ACTIVITY

Symbolism in poetry can be expressed in many ways. An object can represent something more significant. For example, a dove can symbolize peace. A word, action or event also can be symbolic. Write a poem that includes some form of symbolism.

_____

_____

_____

_____

_____

_____

_____

_____

_____

_____

_____

_____

_____

_____

_____

_____

_____

_____

_____

_____

_____

_____

_____

_____

_____

_____
_____
_____
_____
_____
_____
_____
_____
_____
_____
_____
_____
_____
_____
_____
_____
_____
_____
_____
_____
_____
_____
_____
_____
_____

LESSON 17: THE RECKONING

Discussion Questions _____ (10 pts. per question – possible 40 pts.)
Favorite Quote _____ (possible 10 pts.)

Enrichment Activity
    Originality and Creativity   _____ (possible 10 pts.)
    Follows Directions   _____ (possible 10 pts.)
    Language and Style   _____ (possible 10 pts.)
    Composition is Neat   _____ (possible 10 pts.)
    Grammar and Spelling   _____ (possible 10 pts.)

Total Points _____

THE SPELL OF THE YUKON

LESSON 18: QUATRAINS

VOCABULARY

Look for these words in your reading:

Quatrains – a unit or group of four lines of verse
Marionette – a puppet moved by attached strings or wires
Spheral – perfectly rounded
Astral – related to, or coming from the stars

READING

Read: "Quatrains" (Pages 52-53)

DISCUSSION QUESTIONS

1) Why do you think this poem is titled "Quatrains"?

_____

_____

_____

2) What is the difference between the two viewpoints in the poem?

_____

_____

_____

3) Which point of view do you most agree with?

_____

_____

_____

4) How do you think the woman in the poem might respond to the speaker? Write two or three sentences of prose (not poetry) from her point of view.

_____

_____

_____

FAVORITE LINE

What is your favorite line from "Quatrains"? Why?

_____

_____

_____

_____

_____

ENRICHMENT ACTIVITY

Write a quatrain poem following an alternate rhyme scheme (ABAB).

_____

_____

_____

_____

_____

_____

_____

_____

_____

_____

_____

_____

_____

_____

_____

_____

_____

_____

_____

_____

_____

_____

_____

_____

_____

_____

_____

_____

_____

_____
_____
_____
_____
_____
_____
_____
_____
_____
_____
_____
_____
_____
_____
_____
_____
_____
_____
_____
_____
_____
_____
_____

LESSON 18: QUATRAINS

Discussion Questions _____ (10 pts. per question – possible 40 pts.)
Favorite Quote _____ (possible 10 pts.)

Enrichment Activity
    Originality and Creativity   _____ (possible 10 pts.)
    Follows Directions   _____ (possible 10 pts.)
    Language and Style   _____ (possible 10 pts.)
    Composition is Neat   _____ (possible 10 pts.)
    Grammar and Spelling   _____ (possible 10 pts.)

Total Points _____

Fifth- and seventh-grade students created a puppet show for Chitina school children during the 1930s.

Spell of the Yukon Vocabulary
Crossword Puzzle II

Read the Across and Down clues and fill in the blank boxes that match the number on the clues

ACROSS

1 Compel (someone) to go
4 Exhausting work
5 Close friend or associate
8 A strong alcoholic drink
11 To drive away
13 Requested to come
15 To refuse or check sharply
19 Try to acquire or develop (a quality, sentiment or skill)
21 An authoritative command
22 Perfectly rounded
23 Desolate
24 A person who can supposedly see into the future
25 Abandoned ship
26 A puppet moved by attached strings or wires
27 Dismal or gloomy
28 Intensely unpleasant
29 A settling of accounts

DOWN

1 A disk or circle of light shown surrounding or above the head of a saint or holy person to represent their holiness
2 Dislike greatly
3 Work
4 Small edible turtle
6 To avoid something one ought to do
7 A guard whose job is to stand and keep watch
9 Influence
10 Edge
12 To strike with an open hand
14 A person qualified to act as a judge in matters of taste and appreciation
15 State of repentance (feeling sorry for one's sins)
16 Speak irreverently about God or sacred things
17 Related to, or coming from the stars
18 A unit or group of four lines of verse
20 A room or unfinished part of a house just under the roof
24 Severity of nature or manner

Spell of the Yukon Vocabulary
Crossword Puzzle II

Read the Across and Down clues and fill in the blank boxes that match the number on the clues

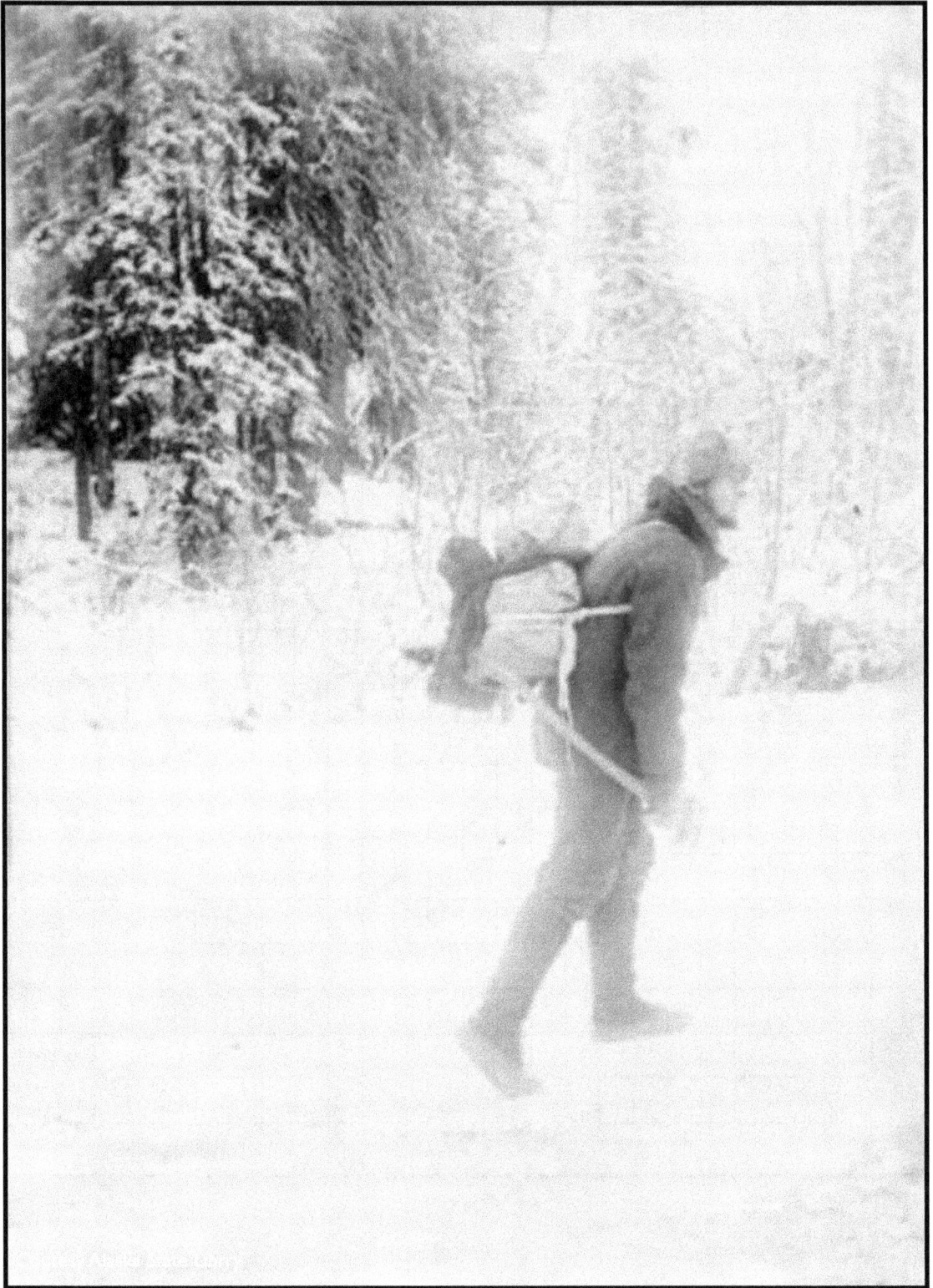

THE SPELL OF THE YUKON

LESSON 19: THE MEN THAT DON'T FIT IN

VOCABULARY

Look for these words in your reading:

Kith and kin – familiar friends, neighbors or relatives
Prime – the most active, thriving or satisfying stage or period

READING

Read: "The Men That Don't Fit In" (Pages 54-55)

DISCUSSION QUESTIONS

1) Describe the men that don't fit in.

_____

_____

_____

2) Why will the "men that don't fit in" never win the race? Who will win the race?

_____

_____

_____

3) What do you notice about the rhyme scheme of this poem?

_____

_____

_____

4) In what ways can you relate to this poem?

_____

_____

_____

FAVORITE LINE

What is your favorite line from "The Men That Don't Fit In"? Why?

_____

_____

_____

_____

_____

ENRICHMENT ACTIVITY

Write a poem from the point of view of a person, animal or object that feels that it doesn't fit in.

_____

_____

_____

_____

_____

_____

_____

_____

_____

_____

_____

_____

_____

_____

_____

_____

_____

_____

_____

_____

_____

_____

_____

_____

_____

_____

_____

_____

_____

_____

_____

_____

_____

_____

_____

_____

_____

_____

_____

_____

_____

_____

_____

_____

_____

_____

_____

_____

_____

LESSON 19: THE MEN THAT DON'T FIT IN

Discussion Questions _____ (10 pts. per question – possible 40 pts.)
Favorite Quote _____ (possible 10 pts.)

Enrichment Activity
 Originality and Creativity   _____ (possible 10 pts.)
 Follows Directions   _____ (possible 10 pts.)
 Language and Style   _____ (possible 10 pts.)
 Composition is Neat   _____ (possible 10 pts.)
 Grammar and Spelling   _____ (possible 10 pts.)

Total Points _____

THE SPELL OF THE YUKON
LESSON 20: MUSIC IN THE BUSH

VOCABULARY

Look for these words in your reading:

Tremulous – shaking or quivering slightly
Listless – too tired or too little interested to want to do things
Melodious – pleasing to the ear because of melody
Vagrant – a person without a settled home or regular work who wanders from place to
   place

READING

Read: "Music in the Bush" (Pages 56-57)

DISCUSSION QUESTIONS

1) What are five words to describe the woman in the poem?

_____
_____
_____

2) Choose the word that best describes the mood of this poem: romantic, sorrowful or
humorous.

_____
_____
_____

3) How do the words used in this poem affect the mood of the poem?

_____
_____
_____

4) What images come to mind as you read this poem?

_____
_____
_____

FAVORITE LINE

What is your favorite line from "Music in the Bush"? Why?

_____
_____
_____
_____
_____

ENRICHMENT ACTIVITY

Write a poem that expresses one of the following moods: optimistic, sorrowful or humorous.

_____
_____
_____
_____
_____
_____
_____
_____
_____
_____
_____
_____
_____
_____
_____
_____
_____
_____
_____
_____
_____
_____
_____
_____
_____

_____
_____
_____
_____
_____
_____
_____
_____
_____
_____
_____
_____
_____
_____
_____
_____
_____
_____
_____
_____
_____
_____
_____
_____

LESSON 20: MUSIC IN THE BUSH

Discussion Questions _____ (10 pts. per question – possible 40 pts.)
Favorite Quote _____ (possible 10 pts.)

Enrichment Activity
    Originality and Creativity   _____ (possible 10 pts.)
    Follows Directions   _____ (possible 10 pts.)
    Language and Style   _____ (possible 10 pts.)
    Composition is Neat   _____ (possible 10 pts.)
    Grammar and Spelling   _____ (possible 10 pts.)

Total Points _____

THE SPELL OF THE YUKON

LESSON 21: RHYME OF THE REMITTANCE MAN

VOCABULARY

Look for these words in your reading:

Remittance – money spent especially in payment
Gilded – covered thinly with gold leaf or gold paint
Vivid – very strong or bright
Rapture – a strong feeling of joy, delight or love

READING

Read: "Rhyme of the Remittance Man" (Pages 58-59)

DISCUSSION QUESTIONS

1) What is the setting of "Rhyme of the Remittance Man"?

_____

_____

_____

2) Who is the speaker?

_____

_____

_____

3) Explain what the following line means: "He is one of us no longer — let him be."

_____

_____

_____

4) What do you think about this poem? Did you enjoy it? Why or why not?

_____

_____

_____

FAVORITE LINE

What is your favorite line from "Rhyme of the Remittance Man"? Why?

_____

_____

_____

_____

_____

ENRICHMENT ACTIVITY

Paraphrase "Rhyme of the Remittance Man" in one or two paragraphs for someone who has not read the poem. Include all of the important details in your own words.

_____

_____

_____

_____

_____

_____

_____

_____

_____

_____

_____

_____

_____

_____

_____

_____

_____

_____

_____

_____

_____

_____

_____

_____

_____

_____

_____

_____

_____

_____

_____

_____

_____

_____

_____

_____

_____

_____

_____

_____

_____

_____

_____

_____

_____

_____

_____

_____

_____

_____

_____

_____

LESSON 21: RHYME OF THE REMITTANCE MAN

Discussion Questions _____ (10 pts. per question – possible 40 pts.)
Favorite Quote _____ (possible 10 pts.)
Enrichment Activity (possible 50 pts.)

Total Points _____

THE SPELL OF THE YUKON

LESSON 22: THE LOW-DOWN WHITE

VOCABULARY

Look for these words in your reading:

Haggard – very thin especially from great hunger, worry or pain
Squalid – extremely dirty and unpleasant
Rogue – a mischievous individual
Bleak – dreary

READING

Read: "The Low-Down White" (Pages 60-61)

DISCUSSION QUESTIONS

1) Do you think that the speaker in this poem is happy with his life? Why or why not?

_____

_____

_____

2) How would you describe the tone of "The Low-Down White"?

_____

_____

_____

3) What rhyme scheme is used in this poem?

_____

_____

_____

4) What did you think about this poem? Did you enjoy it? Why or why not?

_____

_____

_____

FAVORITE LINE

What is your favorite line from "The Low-Down White"? Why?

_____
_____
_____
_____
_____

ENRICHMENT ACTIVITY

What are your three favorite poems (either from this class or elsewhere)? What elements do your favorite poems have in common? Do you relate to the subject matter in some way? Are there similarities in the structure, pattern or tone of the poems? Write your answers below.

_____
_____
_____
_____
_____
_____
_____
_____
_____
_____
_____
_____
_____
_____
_____
_____
_____
_____
_____
_____
_____
_____
_____
_____

_____

_____

_____

_____

_____

_____

_____

_____

_____

_____

_____

_____

_____

_____

_____

_____

_____

_____

_____

_____

_____

_____

_____

_____

_____

_____

_____

_____

_____

LESSON 22: THE LOW-DOWN WHITE

Discussion Questions _____ (10 pts. per question – possible 40 pts.)
Favorite Quote _____ (possible 10 pts.)
Enrichment Activity _____ (possible 50 pts.)

Total Points _____

THE SPELL OF THE YUKON
LESSON 23: THE LITTLE OLD LOG CABIN

VOCABULARY

Look for these words in your reading:

Gouges – to cut holes or grooves in with or as if with a gouge
Solemn – being serious and dignified in appearance or behavior

READING

Read: "The Little Old Log Cabin" (Pages 62-63)

DISCUSSION QUESTIONS

1) Did you have any difficulty understanding "The Little Old Log Cabin"? What are some things that you can do to make a poem easier to understand?

_____
_____
_____

2) How does the dialect affect the meaning and tone of the poem?

_____
_____
_____

3) What does the little old log cabin represent to the speaker?

_____
_____
_____

4) In what ways can you relate to this poem?

_____
_____
_____

FAVORITE LINE

What is your favorite line from "The Little Old Cabin"? Why?

_____

_____

_____

_____

_____

ENRICHMENT ACTIVITY

Using the answers from your enrichment activity in Lesson 22, write a poem using at least one of the characteristics of your favorite poems.

_____

_____

_____

_____

_____

_____

_____

_____

_____

_____

_____

_____

_____

_____

_____

_____

_____

_____

_____

_____

_____

_____

_____

_____

_____

_____

_____

_____

_____

_____

_____

_____

_____

_____

_____

_____

_____

_____

_____

_____

_____

_____

_____

_____

_____

_____

_____

_____

_____

_____

LESSON 23: THE LITTLE OLD LOG CABIN

Discussion Questions _____ (10 pts. per question – possible 40 pts.)
Favorite Quote _____ (possible 10 pts.)

Enrichment Activity
    Originality and Creativity   _____ (possible 10 pts.)
    Follows Directions   _____ (possible 10 pts.)
    Language and Style   _____ (possible 10 pts.)
    Composition is Neat   _____ (possible 10 pts.)
    Grammar and Spelling   _____ (possible 10 pts.)

Total Points _____

THE SPELL OF THE YUKON

LESSON 24: THE YOUNGER SON

VOCABULARY

Look for these words in your reading:

Stalwart – marked by outstanding strength and vigor of mind, body or spirit
Sombre – dismal, gloomy, sad
Argent – resembling silver
In the lurch – leave in a vulnerable and unsupported position

READING

Read: "The Younger Son" (Pages 65-67)

DISCUSSION QUESTIONS

1) In what continent does "The Younger Son" take place? Hint: Look for clues in the first stanza on Page 66.

_____

_____

_____

2) Describe the younger son.

_____

_____

_____

3) How does the speaker feel about the younger son?

_____

_____

_____

4) Which image in the poem stands out to you the most? Why?

_____

_____

_____

FAVORITE LINE

What is your favorite line from "The Younger Son"? Why?

_____
_____
_____
_____
_____

ENRICHMENT ACTIVITY

Write a poem from the point of view of the younger son. Consider how he might feel about his life. Consider what he might say to his family in England.

_____
_____
_____
_____
_____
_____
_____
_____
_____
_____
_____
_____
_____
_____
_____
_____
_____
_____
_____
_____
_____
_____
_____
_____
_____
_____

_____
_____
_____
_____
_____
_____
_____
_____
_____
_____
_____
_____
_____
_____
_____
_____
_____
_____
_____
_____
_____
_____
_____

LESSON 24: THE YOUNGER SON

Discussion Questions _____ (10 pts. per question – possible 40 pts.)
Favorite Quote _____ (possible 10 pts.)

Enrichment Activity
    Originality and Creativity   _____ (possible 10 pts.)
    Follows Directions   _____ (possible 10 pts.)
    Language and Style   _____ (possible 10 pts.)
    Composition is Neat   _____ (possible 10 pts.)
    Grammar and Spelling   _____ (possible 10 pts.)

Total Points _____

THE SPELL OF THE YUKON

LESSON 25: THE MARCH OF THE DEAD

VOCABULARY

Look for these words in your reading:

Triumph – a military victory or conquest
Bunting – a thin cloth used chiefly for making flags and patriotic decorations
Gaunt – lean and haggard, especially because of suffering, hunger, or age
Writhing – to twist and turn this way and that

READING

Read: "The March of the Dead" (Pages 68-70)

DISCUSSION QUESTIONS

1) What is the theme of "The March of the Dead."

_____

_____

_____

2) How would you describe this poem to someone that hasn't read it?

_____

_____

_____

3) How does the use of imagery affect the meaning and tone of this poem?

_____

_____

_____

4) How did you feel after reading this poem? What words describe your emotions?

_____

_____

_____

FAVORITE LINE

What is your favorite line from "The March of the Dead"? Why?

_____

_____

_____

_____

_____

ENRICHMENT ACTIVITY

Write a poem that changes tone. For example, your poem can begin with a humorous tone and shift to a serious tone. Focus on using imagery to create your intended tones.

_____

_____

_____

_____

_____

_____

_____

_____

_____

_____

_____

_____

_____

_____

_____

_____

_____

_____

_____

_____

_____

_____

_____

_____

_____

_____

_____

_____
_____
_____
_____
_____
_____
_____
_____
_____
_____
_____
_____
_____
_____
_____
_____
_____
_____
_____
_____
_____
_____
_____

LESSON 25: THE MARCH OF THE DEAD

Discussion Questions _____ (10 pts. per question – possible 40 pts.)
Favorite Quote _____ (possible 10 pts.)

Enrichment Activity
    Originality and Creativity   _____ (possible 10 pts.)
    Follows Directions   _____ (possible 10 pts.)
    Language and Style   _____ (possible 10 pts.)
    Composition is Neat   _____ (possible 10 pts.)
    Grammar and Spelling   _____ (possible 10 pts.)

Total Points _____

THE SPELL OF THE YUKON

LESSON 26: 'FIGHTING MAC' A LIFE TRAGEDY

VOCABULARY

Look for these words in your reading:

Spectre – something that bothers the mind
Pibroch – a set of variations for the Scottish bagpipe
Flouts – ignore or disregard
Rapine – the violent seizure of someone's property

READING

Read: "'Fighting Mac' A Life Tragedy" (Pages 71-73)

DISCUSSION QUESTIONS

1) Why do you think that Robert Service titled the poem "A Life Tragedy"?

_____

_____

_____

2) What do you notice about the rhyme scheme of this poem?

_____

_____

_____

3) Alliteration is a literary device in which a number of words begin with the same consonant sound close together. It adds musical effect to the work that makes it more pleasurable to read. Here's one example from William Shakespeare's Romeo and Juliet: "From forth the fatal loins of these two foes; a pair of star-cross'd lovers take their life." Shakespeare's repeated use of fs and ls in these lines is an example of alliteration.

What are two examples of alliteration in "'Fighting Mac' A Life Tragedy"?

_____

_____

_____

_____

_____

_____

4) In what ways can you relate to this poem?

_____

_____

_____

FAVORITE LINE

What is your favorite line from "'Fighting Mac' A Life Tragedy"? Why?

_____

_____

_____

_____

_____

ENRICHMENT ACTIVITY

Understanding the historical places, events and people referenced in a poem can help you understand the meaning of the poem. Take some time to research the following list of people and events and write your notes below.

1) Fighting Mac 2) Rob Roy 3) Roderick Dhu 4) Boer War 5) Battle of Magersfontein

After your research, reread the poem. Did you gain greater insight into the meaning of the poem?

_____

_____

_____

_____

_____

_____

_____

_____

_____

_____

_____

_____

_____

_____

_____
_____
_____
_____
_____
_____
_____
_____
_____
_____
_____
_____
_____
_____
_____
_____
_____
_____
_____
_____
_____
_____
_____
_____
_____
_____
_____
_____
_____

LESSON 26: 'FIGHTING MAC' A LIFE TRAGEDY

Discussion Questions _____ (10 pts. per question – possible 40 pts.)
Favorite Quote _____ (possible 10 pts.)
Enrichment Activity _____ (possible 50 pts.)

Total Points _____

THE SPELL OF THE YUKON

LESSON 27: THE WOMAN AND THE ANGEL

VOCABULARY

Look for these words in your reading:

Doffed – to remove or take off

Celestial – of relating to, or suggesting heaven

Scruples – a moral consideration or rule of conduct that makes one uneasy or makes action difficult

Beguiled – deceived by cunning means

READING

Read: "The Woman and the Angel" (Pages 74-75)

DISCUSSION QUESTIONS

1) What did you think that poem was about after you read the title? How did this compare to what the poem really was about?

_____

_____

_____

2) Summarize "The Woman and the Angel" in one sentence.

_____

_____

_____

3) What do you notice about the rhyme scheme of this poem?

_____

_____

_____

4) Can you draw any conclusions about the poet's feelings about human morality from this poem?

_____

_____

_____

FAVORITE LINE

What is your favorite line from "The Woman and the Angel"? Why?

_____

_____

_____

_____

_____

ENRICHMENT ACTIVITY

"The Woman and the Angel" is an example of a couplet (AABB) rhyme scheme. Write your own poem that follows this rhyme scheme.

_____

_____

_____

_____

_____

_____

_____

_____

_____

_____

_____

_____

_____

_____

_____

_____

_____

_____

_____

_____

_____

_____

_____

_____

_____

_____

_____

_____

_____

_____

_____

_____

_____

_____

_____

_____

_____

_____

_____

_____

_____

_____

_____

_____

_____

_____

LESSON 27: THE WOMAN AND THE ANGEL

Discussion Questions _____ (10 pts. per question – possible 40 pts.)
Favorite Quote _____ (possible 10 pts.)

Enrichment Activity
    Originality and Creativity   _____ (possible 10 pts.)
     Follows Directions   _____ (possible 10 pts.)
     Language and Style   _____ (possible 10 pts.)
     Composition is Neat   _____ (possible 10 pts.)
     Grammar and Spelling   _____ (possible 10 pts.)

Total Points _____

THE SPELL OF THE YUKON
LESSON 28: THE RHYME OF THE RESTLESS ONES

VOCABULARY

Look for these words in your reading:

Stagnation – to become motionless
Roam – to go from place to place without purpose or direction
Serf – a slave bound to a certain piece of land
Blot out – to make obscure, insignificant or inconsequential

READING

Read: "The Rhyme of the Restless Ones" (Pages 76-77)

DISCUSSION QUESTIONS

1) Describe the "restless ones" in your own words.

_____

_____

_____

2) Which Robert Service poem has a similar theme to "The Rhyme of the Restless Ones"?

_____

_____

_____

3) Explain the following stanza in your own words:
      No, there's that in us that time can never tame;
      And life will always seem a careless game;
      And they'd better far forget —
      Those who say they love us yet —
      Forget, blot out with bitterness our name.

_____

_____

_____

_____

_____

_____

_____

4) In what ways do you relate to this poem?

_____

_____

_____

FAVORITE LINE

What is your favorite line from "The Rhyme of the Restless Ones"? Why?

_____

_____

_____

_____

_____

ENRICHMENT ACTIVITY

"The Rhyme of the Restless Ones" is an example of a couplet (AABB) rhyme scheme. Write a poem about a time that you felt restless. Incorporate at least two of the vocabulary words from this lesson into your poem.

_____

_____

_____

_____

_____

_____

_____

_____

_____

_____

_____

_____

_____

_____

_____

_____

_____

_____

_____
_____
_____
_____
_____
_____
_____
_____
_____
_____
_____
_____
_____
_____
_____
_____
_____
_____
_____
_____
_____
_____
_____

LESSON 28: THE RHYME OF THE RESTLESS ONES

Discussion Questions _____ (10 pts. per question – possible 40 pts.)
Favorite Quote _____ (possible 10 pts.)

Enrichment Activity
   Originality and Creativity   _____ (possible 10 pts.)
   Follows Directions   _____ (possible 10 pts.)
   Language and Style   _____ (possible 10 pts.)
   Composition is Neat   _____ (possible 10 pts.)
   Grammar and Spelling   _____ (possible 10 pts.)

Total Points _____

THE SPELL OF THE YUKON

LESSON 29: NEW YEAR'S EVE

VOCABULARY

Look for these words in your reading:

Weltering – moving in a turbulent fashion
Ghastly – horrible or shocking
Sodden – dull or lacking in expression
Rouse – to bring out of a state of sleep, unconsciousness, inactivity

READING

Read: "New Year's Eve" (Pages 78-81)

DISCUSSION QUESTIONS

1) Read the poem out loud again. Did you notice anything new that you didn't notice the first time that you read it? If so, what?

_____

_____

_____

2) Are there any instances of anaphora in this poem? If so, which words were repeated?

_____

_____

_____

3) What word best describes the tone of this poem: humorous, serious or gloomy? What are some phrases that support your answer?

_____

_____

_____

_____

4) How did this poem make you feel?

_____

_____

_____

FAVORITE LINE

What is your favorite line from "New Year's Eve"? Why?

_____

_____

_____

_____

_____

ENRICHMENT ACTIVITY

New Year's Eve is typically a time of reflection and making resolutions for the future. Write your own New Year's Eve poem that either reflects on your past or expresses your hopes for the future.

_____

_____

_____

_____

_____

_____

_____

_____

_____

_____

_____

_____

_____

_____

_____

_____

_____

_____

_____

_____

_____

_____

_____

_____
_____
_____
_____
_____
_____
_____
_____
_____
_____
_____
_____
_____
_____
_____
_____
_____
_____
_____
_____
_____
_____
_____

LESSON 29: NEW YEAR'S EVE

Discussion Questions _____ (10 pts. per question – possible 40 pts.)
Favorite Quote _____ (possible 10 pts.)

Enrichment Activity
    Originality and Creativity   _____ (possible 10 pts.)
    Follows Directions   _____ (possible 10 pts.)
    Language and Style   _____ (possible 10 pts.)
    Composition is Neat   _____ (possible 10 pts.)
    Grammar and Spelling   _____ (possible 10 pts.)

Total Points _____

THE SPELL OF THE YUKON
LESSON 30: COMFORT

VOCABULARY

Look for these words in your reading:

Bereft – not having something needed, wanted or expected
Dazzles – blind temporarily
Mope – be dejected and apathetic
Tatters – irregularly torn pieces of cloth

READING

Read: "Comfort" (Page 82)

DISCUSSION QUESTIONS

1) What is the theme of "Comfort"?

_____

_____

_____

2) Who is the audience of this poem?

_____

_____

_____

3) Do you agree with the speaker's advice? Why or why not?

_____

_____

_____

_____

_____

4) What words or phrases stand out to you the most? Why?

_____

_____

_____

FAVORITE LINE

What is your favorite line from "Comfort"? Why?

_____

_____

_____

_____

_____

ENRICHMENT ACTIVITY

Poetry can be used to uplift and encourage your readers. Think of a time that a friend or family member was going through a difficult time. Write a poem to encourage that person.

_____

_____

_____

_____

_____

_____

_____

_____

_____

_____

_____

_____

_____

_____

_____

_____

_____

_____

_____

_____

_____

_____

_____

_____

_____
_____
_____
_____
_____
_____
_____
_____
_____
_____
_____
_____
_____
_____
_____
_____
_____
_____
_____
_____
_____
_____
_____
_____

LESSON 30: COMFORT

Discussion Questions _____ (10 pts. per question – possible 40 pts.)
Favorite Quote _____ (possible 10 pts.)

Enrichment Activity
    Originality and Creativity   _____ (possible 10 pts.)
    Follows Directions   _____ (possible 10 pts.)
    Language and Style   _____ (possible 10 pts.)
    Composition is Neat   _____ (possible 10 pts.)
    Grammar and Spelling   _____ (possible 10 pts.)

Total Points _____

THE SPELL OF THE YUKON
LESSON 31: THE HARPY

VOCABULARY

Look for these words in your reading:

Harpy – slang term for a lady of the night
Iniquity – something that is unjust or wicked; sin
Sate – satisfy (a desire or an appetite) to the fullest
Attainted – affect or infect with disease or corruption

READING

Read: "The Harpy" (Pages 83-85)

DISCUSSION QUESTIONS

1) Why do you think that Robert Service titled this poem "The Harpy"?

_____

_____

_____

2) Summarize the poem in one sentence.

_____

_____

_____

3) How does the rhyme scheme affect the tone and meaning of this poem?

_____

_____

_____

_____

4) Do you think the woman described in this poem is happy? Explain your answer.

_____

_____

_____

FAVORITE LINE

What is your favorite line from "The Harpy"? Why?

_____

_____

_____

_____

_____

ENRICHMENT ACTIVITY

"The Harpy" has a triplet rhyme scheme where every stanza contains three lines that rhyme (AAA). Write a poem that contains at least one stanza of three lines that rhyme.

_____

_____

_____

_____

_____

_____

_____

_____

_____

_____

_____

_____

_____

_____

_____

_____

_____

_____

_____

_____

_____

_____

_____

_____

_____

_____

_____

_____
_____
_____
_____
_____
_____
_____
_____
_____
_____
_____
_____
_____
_____
_____
_____
_____
_____
_____
_____
_____
_____
_____
_____
_____

LESSON 31: THE HARPY

Discussion Questions _____ (10 pts. per question – possible 40 pts.)
Favorite Quote _____ (possible 10 pts.)

Enrichment Activity
    Originality and Creativity   _____ (possible 10 pts.)
    Follows Directions   _____ (possible 10 pts.)
    Language and Style   _____ (possible 10 pts.)
    Composition is Neat   _____ (possible 10 pts.)
    Grammar and Spelling   _____ (possible 10 pts.)

Total Points _____

THE SPELL OF THE YUKON
LESSON 32: PREMONITION

VOCABULARY

Look for these words in your reading:

Premonition – a forewarning
Gibbous – more than half but less than fully illuminated

READING

Read: "Premonition" (Page 86)

DISCUSSION QUESTIONS

1) What is the theme of "Premonition"?

_____
_____
_____

2) Who had a premonition? Who was the premonition about?

_____
_____
_____

3) What line in this poem contains a metaphor (a figure of speech that compares two things that are unrelated but share common characteristics).

_____
_____
_____
_____
_____

4) Have you ever had a premonition? If so, explain.

_____
_____
_____

FAVORITE LINE

What is your favorite line from "Premonition"? Why?

_____

_____

_____

_____

_____

ENRICHMENT ACTIVITY

Metaphors and similes are two literary devices that are often confused:

Metaphor: a figure of speech that compares two things that are unrelated but share common characteristics without the use of "like" or "as"

Simile: a figure of speech which explicitly compares two things that are unrelated using the words "like" or "as"

Write two examples of a metaphor and two examples of a simile from any kind of literature. Then write your own example of a metaphor and a simile.

_____

_____

_____

_____

_____

_____

_____

_____

_____

_____

_____

_____

_____

_____

_____

_____

_____

_____
_____
_____
_____
_____
_____
_____
_____
_____
_____
_____
_____
_____
_____
_____
_____
_____
_____
_____
_____
_____
_____
_____
_____
_____
_____
_____
_____
_____

LESSON 32: PREMONITION

Discussion Questions _____ (10 pts. per question – possible 40 pts.)
Favorite Quote _____ (possible 10 pts.)
Enrichment Activity _____ (possible 50 pts.)

Total Points _____

THE SPELL OF THE YUKON
LESSON 33: THE TRAMPS

VOCABULARY

Look for these words in your reading:

Comrade – an intimate friend or associate
Vassal – someone/something that is subordinate
Jest – a comic act or remark
Exultantly – full of or expressing joy or triumph

READING

Read: "The Tramps" (Page 87)

DISCUSSION QUESTIONS

1) What is the theme of "The Tramps"?

_____

_____

_____

2) Who is the speaker of this poem? Who is the audience?

_____

_____

_____

3) Where do you think the "road to Anywhere" leads?

_____

_____

_____

_____

_____

4) In what ways can you relate to this poem? Explain why.

_____

_____

_____

FAVORITE LINE

What is your favorite line from "The Tramps"? Why?

_____
_____
_____
_____
_____

ENRICHMENT ACTIVITY

Write a poem with the theme of adventure. Include at least two of the vocabulary words from this lesson.

_____
_____
_____
_____
_____
_____
_____
_____
_____
_____
_____
_____
_____
_____
_____
_____
_____
_____
_____
_____
_____
_____
_____
_____
_____

_____
_____
_____
_____
_____
_____
_____
_____
_____
_____
_____
_____
_____
_____
_____
_____
_____
_____
_____
_____
_____
_____
_____
_____
_____
_____

LESSON 33: THE TRAMPS

Discussion Questions _____ (10 pts. per question – possible 40 pts.)
Favorite Quote _____ (possible 10 pts.)

Enrichment Activity
    Originality and Creativity   _____ (possible 10 pts.)
    Follows Directions   _____ (possible 10 pts.)
    Language and Style   _____ (possible 10 pts.)
    Composition is Neat   _____ (possible 10 pts.)
    Grammar and Spelling   _____ (possible 10 pts.)

Total Points _____

THE SPELL OF THE YUKON

LESSON 34: L'ENVOI

VOCABULARY

Look for these words in your reading:

L'envoi – one or more detached verses at the end of a literary composition, serving to convey the moral, or to address the poem to a particular person

Assail – to attack violently with words or blows

Argonauts – a group of heroes who accompanied Jason on board the ship *Argo* in the quest for the Golden Fleece

Vanquishing – to defeat and gain control of completely

READING

Read: "L'envoi" (Pages 88-89)

DISCUSSION QUESTIONS

1) What is the purpose of this poem?

_____

_____

_____

2) What rhyme scheme does Robert Service use in the poem?

_____

_____

_____

3) What literary devices do you notice in the first stanza of this poem?

_____

_____

_____

_____

_____

4) What images came to mind as you read this poem? What words or phrases inspired these images?

_____

_____

_____

FAVORITE LINE

What is your favorite line from "L'envoi"? Why?

_____

_____

_____

_____

_____

ENRICHMENT ACTIVITY

You have now read and analyzed 34 poems by Robert Service. Which one was your favorite? Why? Look over the poems that you wrote for enrichment activities. Which one is your favorite? Why? Write your answers below.

_____

_____

_____

_____

_____

_____

_____

_____

_____

_____

_____

_____

_____

_____

_____

_____

_____

_____

_____

_____

_____

_____

_____

_____

_____

_____
_____
_____
_____
_____
_____
_____
_____
_____
_____
_____
_____
_____
_____
_____
_____
_____
_____
_____
_____
_____
_____
_____
_____
_____
_____

LESSON 34: L'ENVOI

Discussion Questions _____ (10 pts. per question – possible 40 pts.)
Favorite Quote _____ (possible 10 pts.)
Enrichment Activity _____ (possible 50 pts.)

Total Points _____

Robert Service

115

Spell of the Yukon Vocabulary
Crossword Puzzle III

Read the Across and Down clues and fill in the blank boxes that match the number on the clues

ACROSS

2 Very strong or bright
4 Ignore or disregard
7 Someone/something that is subordinate
9 Not having something needed, wanted or expected
12 An intimate friend or associate
15 Be dejected and apathetic
17 A strong feeling of joy, delight or love
18 A slave bound to a certain piece of land
20 Very thin, especially from great hunger, worry or pain
21 Horrible or shocking
25 Marked by outstanding strength and vigor of mind, body or spirit
26 Dull or lacking in expression
28 Too tired or too little interested to want to do things
30 Covered thinly with gold leaf or gold paint

35 To bring out of a state of sleep, unconsciousness, inactivity
36 Affect or infect with disease or corruption
38 The most active, thriving or satisfying stage or period
40 Resembling silver
41 Shaking or quivering slightly
42 Leave in a vulnerable and unsupported position
44 To become motionless
46 Dreary
47 More than half but less than fully illuminated
48 Familiar friends, neighbors or relatives
49 A mischievous individual
50 Of relating to, or suggesting heaven
51 A military victory or conquest
52 A set of variations for the Scottish bagpipe
53 Slang term for a lady of the night
54 Something that bothers the mind
55 To defeat and gain control of completely

DOWN

1 The violent seizure of someone's property
3 To remove or take off
5 Irregularly torn pieces of cloth
6 To go from place to place without purpose or direction
8 Being serious and dignified in appearance or behavior
10 A moral consideration or rule of conduct that makes one uneasy or makes action difficult
11 Blind temporarily
13 A person without a settled home or regular work who wanders from place to place
14 Deceived by cunning means
16 To attack violently with words or blows
19 Extremely dirty and unpleasant

22 A group of heroes who accompanied Jason on board the ship Argo in the quest for the Golden Fleece
23 Pleasing to the ear because of melody
24 One or more detached verses at the end of a literary composition, serving to convey the moral, or to address the poem to a particular person
27 Moving in a turbulent fashion
29 Dismal, gloomy, sad
30 To cut holes or grooves in with or as if with a gouge
31 Something that is unjust or wicked; sin
32 To twist and turn this way and that
33 Lean and haggard, especially because of suffering, hunger, or age
34 A comic act or remark
37 Full of or expressing joy or triumph

Spell of the Yukon Vocabulary
Crossword Puzzle III

Read the Across and Down clues and fill in the blank boxes that match the number on the clues

DOWN - Continued

38 A forewarning
39 Money spent especially in payment
43 Satisfy (a desire or an appetite) to the fullest

45 A thin cloth used chiefly for making flags and patriotic decorations
46 To make obscure, insignificant or inconsequential

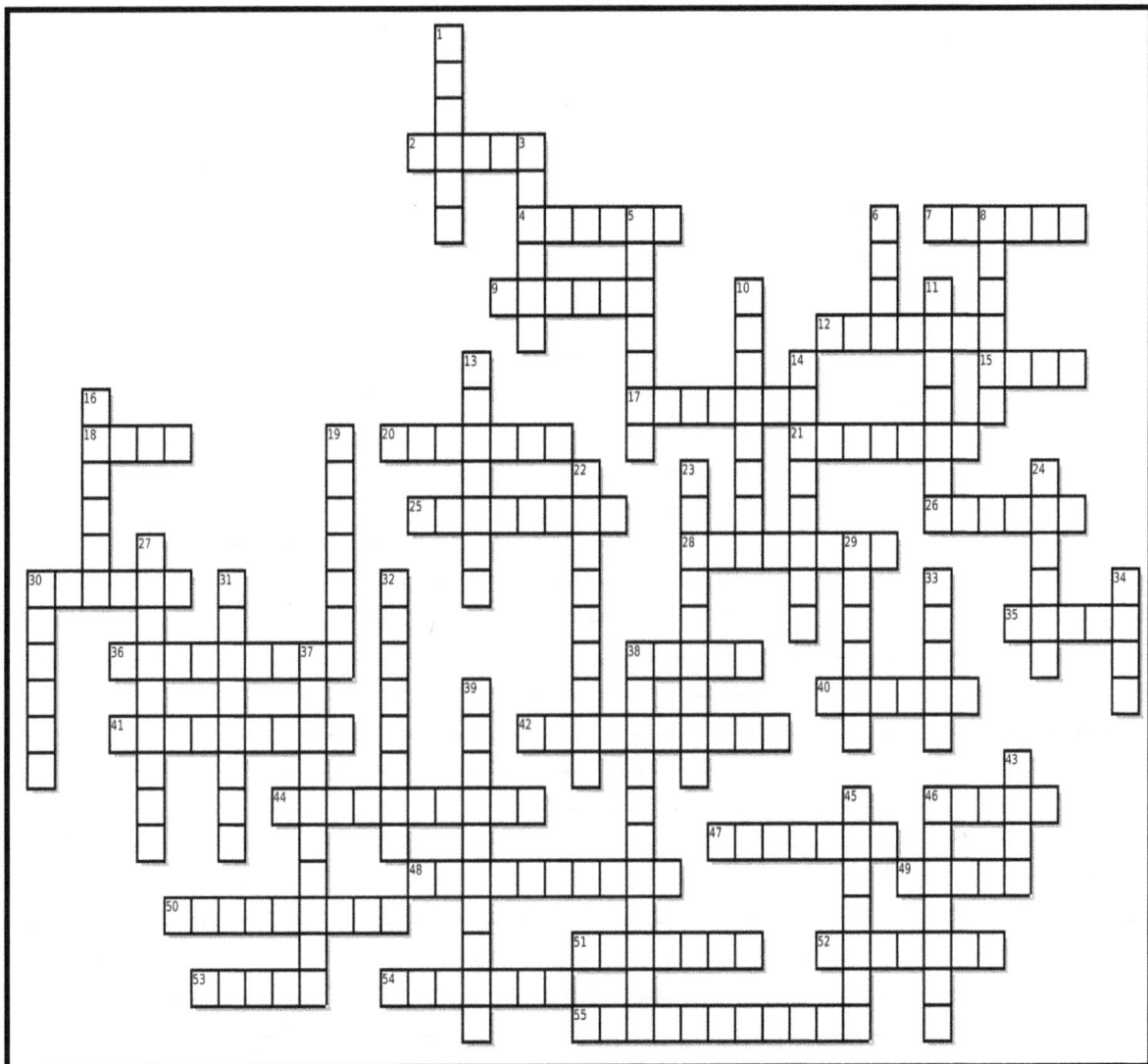

THE SPELL OF THE YUKON

LESSON 35: BARD OF THE YUKON/AFTER THE YUKON

READING

"Bard of the Yukon" (Pages 90-103)
"Life After the Yukon" (Pages 104-114)

ESSAY QUESTIONS

Answer the following questions in paragraph form:

1) What were Robert Service's early years like? How did those expeiences influence his writing?

_____

_____

_____

_____

_____

_____

_____

_____

_____

_____

_____

_____

_____

_____

_____

_____

_____

_____

_____

_____

_____

_____

_____

_____

_____

2) How and why did Robert Service end up in Alaska? How did his time in the Yukon become a turning point in his life? In what ways did it inspire his writing?

_____

_____

_____

_____

_____

_____

_____

_____

_____

_____

_____

_____

_____

_____

_____

_____

_____

_____

_____

_____

_____

_____

_____

_____

_____

_____

_____

_____

_____

_____

_____

3) After reading about the life of Robert Service, what new insights did you gain into his poetry?

_____

_____

_____

_____

_____

_____

_____

_____

_____

_____

_____

_____

_____

_____

_____

_____

_____

_____

_____

_____

_____

_____

_____

_____

_____

_____

_____

_____

_____

_____

_____

_____

_____

_____

_____

_____

_____

LESSON 35: THE BARD OF THE YUKON/AFTER THE YUKON

Lesson 35 contains three essay questions to test your knowledge of the assigned reading. You can earn up to 20 points for each essay. And you will be graded on a scale of 1-5 in four categories:

1) Understanding the topic
2) Answering all questions completely and accurately
3) Neatness and organization
4) Grammar, spelling and punctuation

Use the essay rubric grid as a guide to earn up to 5 points in each category for every essay.

Essay 1

Demonstrates understanding of the topic   _____ (possible 5 pts.)
Answered the questions completely and accurately   _____ (possible 5 pts.)
Composition is neat   _____ (possible 5 pts.)
Grammar and Spelling   _____ (possible 5 pts.)

          Total _____

Essay 2

Demonstrates understanding of the topic   _____ (possible 5 pts.)
Answered the questions completely and accurately   _____ (possible 5 pts.)
Composition is neat   _____ (possible 5 pts.)
Grammar and Spelling   _____ (possible 5 pts.)

          Total _____

Essay 3

Demonstrates understanding of the topic   _____ (possible 5 pts.)
Answered the questions completely and accurately   _____ (possible 5 pts.)
Composition is neat   _____ (possible 5 pts.)
Grammar and Spelling   _____ (possible 5 pts.)

          Total _____

Rubric for Poetry Enrichment Assignments

	Beginning 2	Needs Improvement 4	Acceptable 6	Accomplished 8	Exemplary 10
Originality and Creativity	Student made no attempt to write a creative or original piece	Student attempted to focus on the assigned theme, but lacks creativity	Student's work shows some creativity and originality	Student's work is creative, original and on topic	Student took ownership of the assignment to make it his/her own original piece
Follows Directions	Student made no attempt to follow the directions	Student attempted to follow directions but lacks understanding of the given topic/style	Student mostly followed the instructions	Student's poem is written according to the directions	Student's poem demonstrates strong understanding of the topic/style
Word Choice and Style	Student's writing is confusing and lacks personal style	Student's work is clear, but lacks personal style	Student's work is clear and shows some personal style	Student's word choice and style is effective and appropriate	Student uses expressive style and sophisticated word choice
Neatness	Student's work is sloppy	Student's work is somewhat neat	Student's essay is mostly neat	Student's work is neat	Student demonstrates extra care making it neat
Grammar and Spelling	Student's work contains several grammar and spelling mistakes which makes it hard to understand	Student's work contains some grammar, spelling and punctuation mistakes, but not enough to impede understanding	Student's work contains only 1 or 2 grammar, spelling or punctuation errors	Student's work contains no grammar, spelling or punctuation errors	Student's work is extremely well-written

Rubric for Essay Questions (Lesson 35)

	Beginning 1	Needs Improvement 2	Acceptable 3	Accomplished 4	Exemplary 5
Demonstrates Understanding of the Topic	Student's work shows incomplete understanding of the topic	Student's work shows slight understanding of the topic	Student's work shows a basic understanding of the topic	Student's work shows complete understanding of the topic	Student's work demonstrates strong insight about the topic
Answered questions completely and accurately	Student's work did not address all of the questions	Student answered all of the questions with some accuracy	Student answered all questions with close to 100% accuracy	Student answered all questions with 100% accuracy	Student goes beyond the questions to demonstrate knowledge of the topic
Essay is neat and well organized	Student's work is sloppy and unorganized	Student's work is somewhat neat and organized	Student's essay is neat and somewhat organized	Student's work is well organized and neat	Student demonstrates extra care in organizing the essay and making it neat
Essay contains good grammar and spelling	Student's work is poorly written and hard to understand	Student's work contains some grammar, spelling and punctuation mistakes, but not enough to impede understanding	Student's work contains only 1 or 2 grammar, spelling or punctuation errors	Student's work contains no grammar, spelling or punctuation errors	Student's work is extremely well-written